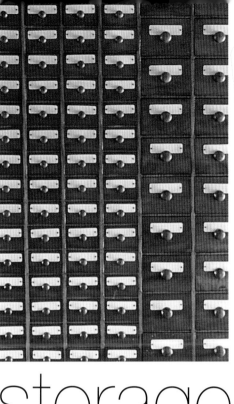

storage

storage

recipes and ideas

Kasha Harmer Hirst

CHRONICLE BOOKS

SAN FRANCISCO

First published in the United States in 2001 by Chronicle Books

Editorial Director: Jane O'Shea
Consultant Art Director: Helen Lewis
Project Editor: Nicki Marshall
Design Assistant: Sarah Emery
Production: Sarah Tucker
Special Photography: Richard Foster
Styling: Kasha Harmer Hirst
Picture Researcher: Nadine Bazar
Illustrations: Carolyn Jenkins

Text © 2001 Kasha Harmer Hirst
Design & Layout © 2001 Quadrille Publishing Ltd

Printed and bound in Hong Kong

Interior design and layout by Quadrille Publishing
Cover Design by Kirsten Hetland

Distributed in Canada by Raincoast Books
9050 Shaughnessy Street
Vancouver, British Columbia V6P 6E5

10 9 8 7 6 5 4 3 2 1

Chronicle Books LLC
85 Second Street
San Francisco, California 94105

www.chroniclebooks.com

Publisher's note

When following instructions for the projects, check the
Practicalities section at the back of the book for full
measurements and helpful illustrations. Throughout the book
measurements are given in both metric and imperial. When
following any of the methods described use either all metric or all
imperial, as the two are not necessarily interchangeable.

contents

1

introduction

While it may just be possible to be too rich or too thin, you can never have too much storage space. Good storage is both the art and science of making space work—beautifully. It makes the house a living machine, customized to fulfill the specific needs of our individual lives. If we are to meet the various demands the world makes of us, we need to come from a position of strength. Only if we have some degree of order and calm at home can we be focused enough to conquer all. If the rising tide of paper on your office floor threatens to drown you, if kitchen or bathroom cabinets start to strain under ten types of oil or twenty types of moisturizer, if it becomes impossible to do the ironing because you can't find the iron, then it is time to take control and organize your life.

While some cultures carry their worldly goods on their back, we in the West tend to accumulate and hoard.

According to Feng Shui (and common sense), areas of clutter cause stagnant energy. The psychological effects of keeping your house in order should not be underestimated. Take a critical look around you and evaluate what you have—then edit it wherever possible. Give space a value and keep only what is necessary. Trash any excess baggage or give it to charity—paring down is good for the soul.

Efficient storage is desirable whether you live in a farmhouse or an urban studio, but is especially crucial where space is at a premium. After all, space is money (which is perhaps easier to understand in a city, where it is about the most expensive thing that you can buy). Those who want to live without walls in large, undivided loft spaces, where every "zone" is constantly on view, have to be especially organized as there is an extra strain on storage. By "streamlining" our homes, we are actually getting rid of all those hardworking

There is no room for clutter in a space where the architecture is clean and spare. The pull-out shelving unit in this room blends almost seamlessly into the wall when closed.

In a large bedroom, the sleeping area is divided off from the rest of the room by a partition wall built deep enough to take shelving for books and bedside accessories.

Besides providing storage, a beautiful collection of boxes of various shapes and sizes can make an effective display. These distinctive orange boxes are trophies from Hermés.

areas that in the past supported the primary spaces. Despite dumping the antimacassars and the figurines, we all seem to have more possessions than our ancestors ever dreamed of, and fewer rooms to keep them in (R.I.P. the pantry, the attic, the utility room). So where to stow it all?

Although hardworking storage requires conscious planning, there is no real secret to it—all the rules are based on innate common sense. You probably won't even have deliberated them consciously because they seem so apparent, but by focusing on them and relating them to the specifics of your situation you will discover the logical solutions. So, going over the basics again will be useful.

Invest a few hours (payback time will come) evaluating your needs and deciding what you use and when and where you use it. Things that you need often should be easily accessible and placed at hand or eye level, while you can afford to keep items that are used only rarely on a very high or low shelf and toward the back of a cabinet or drawer. In the bedroom, plan to make for your underwear more often than your evening wear; in the kitchen, make the double boiler more accessible than the fish kettle. If you haven't used something at all over the past year, seriously consider whether it merits the space that it currently occupies. If not, either chuck it out or pass it on.

If this seems like the last way you'd ever want to spend a weekend, then do it bit by bit—you don't have to sort it all out at once in a giant spring cleaning. When you know what you need to store, you can decide what storage you need. Do any of your possessions merit display, or would you prefer them to be hidden from view? Books warrant open shelves to invite readers, clothing a closet which protects from dust, while collections (from figurines to fossils) demand limelight and the room to expand. Use shallow drawers or shelves for smaller items so that they don't get lost in the space, while bulkier pieces will need deeper, stronger furniture. Be creative with your space.

1. The storage system is part of the architecture in this apartment. The recessed modular shelving, built out from the wall, suits objects of all shapes and sizes and leaves the space virtually clutter-free. A system of sliding doors streamlines the space even further.

2. Nothing but the task at hand is in evidence in this home office: a comprehensive system of built-in cabinets and drawers, custom-made to suit the shape of the space, provides adequate storage for all other items.

1 Here, box drawers have been recessed into an original alcove.

2 Rows of shelving fitted between two structural supports makes clever use of space.

3 A large cabinet floats in this open plan space. The cabinet can be accessed from each living zone and stores relevant clothing and equipment. Here, in the bedroom it is used as a wardrobe.

Built-in storage is generally more space efficient than freestanding, but it takes foresight and resolve to dedicate expensive square feet of living space to storage. Besides, the evolving demands made of a space (a change of use because of a growing family, for example) can make the construction of additional closets of cabinets too much of a commitment. Also to overcome are the twin headaches of cost and finding a decent contractor. Freestanding storage may be less efficient, but it is infinitely more flexible and can easily be relocated, removed or supplemented with other pieces. The relative merits of built-in and freestanding storage depend a great deal on the room in question. In a kitchen, fitted cabinets will usually provide most of the storage. In a bedroom, the existing closet is usually adequate for hanging garments and storing shoes, while freestanding furniture, such as a dressing table and chest of drawers, takes care of

other items. In a living room, the addition of some built-in cabinets and shelves will often make the room more inviting by organizing possessions in a coherent, attractive way. When designing built-in units, consider the proportions of a room, so that you don't end up making a short room shorter or a narrow room narrower.

Efficient storage is even more of a must if you have kids. They may be small, but their needs are large. The closet will be most useful if fitted with some shelves, since children's clothes tend to be designed to fold rather than hang. A large toy box (preferably on casters) is indispensable if you have children, as the debris of the day can be swept into it.

Style will also affect your storage choices. You know if you're a traditionalist or modernist, if you feel more at home with an old-fashioned wooden wardrobe or an industrial, shop-standard, freestanding clothes-rail. But try not to compromise efficiency for an aesthetic—think function before decoration. If you hanker after minimalism, remember that it is a philosophy as well as an aesthetic. The true minimalist edits possessions down to the bare but beautiful essentials, not simply shoving all the paraphernalia of life into closets and behind false walls.

Smart storage isn't about being obsessive or controlling, about keeping your drawers filed regimentally. It is about making intelligent use of space to free yourself from all that constant searching: from sifting shelves of turtle necks to get at a bikini; from wading through piles of papers just to find an address. We are all time-hungry, and sorted storage buys us time. Your home won't just work better, it will look better, too. There will always be room for a little picturesque clutter—just don't be its victim.

Storage is about streamlining, about adapting your space to accommodate how you live—not boring but beautiful. In these pages you'll find innovative storage solutions for each area of the home and several specific storage projects with easy to follow directions. Consult the practicalities section at the back of the book for detailed information on materials and techniques.

1 A large cabinet divides a large room into separate zones. When it is closed, all that is evident are the ceramics displayed within the glass-fronted niches, offering a decorative focus within the room.

2 When the cabinet is open, the user can access the interior usually hidden from view. With a variety of heights and widths, the shelves are able to accommodate a diverse collection of items, from dishes to stationery. This is a clever combination of display cabinet and closed shelving in one.

3 Glass shelving preserves a feeling of light in this tiny attic kitchen-dining room. More storage for kitchen utensils is provided in the more solid under-counter cabinets.

2

recipes and ideas

The living room is traditionally the place where people spend much of their leisure time at home. By definition the most multi-functional room in the house, and the most social, the living room has to accommodate a wide variety of possessions including books, the television, a music system, and any collections, either stored away or on display. If the kitchen is the heart of the home, then this is its soul.

living rooms

Depending on its size, who you are, and how you live, you might use your living room to rest, read, play, party, or just hang out and lounge. How do you use yours? Do you end up eating in here from a low coffee table rather than in a kitchen or dining room? Do you enjoy reading or watching television or films, or do you prefer to listen to music or meditate? You may have children and animals to share your time and space with, games and equipment to store, or letters to write. How demanding of your space are you?

1. The storage system spans the whole wall and comprises both closed and open storage, which makes it perfect for a variety of objects. The niches provide a jigsaw of display and useful storage for home entertainment systems, while the adjoining bookshelves house the wet bar and the library.

2. Shelves and drawers have been built into a redundant chimney and are normally concealed with hinged sliding doors.

A living room usually has to satisfy the needs of more than one individual, which can make planning difficult. In addition, this is the area of the house most frequently seen by visitors—so it is important that it be relatively ordered while still exuding comfort. Storage solutions here will be necessarily complex, enabling you to stash away or display all your favorite possessions while maintaining the essential aura of calm.

Few homes now have the luxury of a dedicated dining room. Instead meals are taken, either formally or informally, in the kitchen or living room. This trend presents its own storage requirements. The sideboard is enjoying a well-deserved revival and is the perfect place to store any overflow of glass and tableware from the kitchen—and looks just as good in a living space as it did in the dining room. It can also be used to display family photographs or favorite artwork and can serve as a liquor cabinet.

Once you have assessed which items require storage, you can decide which solutions best answer your needs. If you have a sizable library, a built-in bookcase will spread the load and make the most of all available space. Make sure that the shelves are fixed soundly to structurally solid walls and have adequate supports at suitable intervals. A passionate reader will probably need to position a lamp by the side of any favorite seat, and a side table or shelf nearby on which to keep current reading matter and rest a glass. Think about choosing a coffee table with a shelf or rack underneath for extra magazine and newspaper storage.

1 This library is arranged within an open living space and is used to separate the living area from the kitchen behind. Its design keeps the books both accessible and out of the way.

2 Ron Arad's now-classic "bookworm" decorates the wall, stores reading matter for those seated beneath, and brings a touch of the contemporary to a period house.

3 This extensive music collection is kept hidden away yet close at hand in specially designed drawers. Each drawer can be pulled right out, so that every CD can be seen at a glance.

If music seems to sound better when you're relaxing in comfort on a sofa, then try to position the music system nearby and the speakers away from each other. A television cabinet may sound like an old-fashioned option, but they are not all reproduction nightmares. They can be desirable pieces of furniture in their own right and will also provide storage for all the other home entertainment paraphernalia. But why hide the television set when streamlined design has reinvented it as a modern object of desire—the centerpiece of the 21st-century home—with a choice of designs ranging from the ultra slim, which can be fixed flat to a wall, to the ultra light, which can be carried from room to room.

One fairly successful solution is to dedicate an entire wall to open and closed shelving that is flexible enough to house everything from a vase of flowers to your collection of films. This cuts down on multiple pieces of furniture and keeps the whole room focused toward one area—and is relatively easy to keep ordered. If your living space is open plan or multipurpose, taking in parts of what were traditionally separate rooms—for example, if they include a dining table, study area or even a kitchen—you can use storage components that will either clearly demarcate the different zones or be flexible enough to serve a number of different functions.

Once you have mentally subdivided your space into separate areas for different tasks, where to store things will become obvious. Tailor your storage to your requirements, and the space, while making sure that your room does not end up looking overly utilitarian with too many disparate elements and no decorative focus. No matter how well organized, a space that looks like an office will hardly be an easy place in which to unwind or entertain.

This is the room where a lot of the junk of everyday life ends up, from loose change to old newspapers, so edit it—regularly. Remember that space, a visual pause, is the greatest luxury of all.

1 A set of bookshelves that run from wall to wall becomes part of the architecture of this space and brings order to chaos. Creating the shelves from the same material that was used for the floor increases visual harmony.

2 These revolving rails, based on ships' sails, store books on one side and display artwork on the other. They can act as room dividers between a living and dining area or can be rotated to open up the space.

Portrait of a room

Open-plan spaces can pose particular storage problems. In
this loft apartment, a large unit acts as a partition wall between
the main living area and the kitchen and hall space beyond.
The unit has been specially designed to provide an integral
home office and the maximum amount of storage space
possible for all of the living room essentials—including home
entertainment equipment and collections, which are stored on
open shelving and drawers. A fully-equipped home office is
fitted on the right-hand side of the unit, with every storage
requirement catered for. Because the unit has a pull-down
sliding door, everything can be hidden away when not in use to
leave a calm, seamless front in keeping with the space.

Low-level Seat Cabinets

Cupboards around the wall create seating and storage

In this room, low-level cabinets are positioned all the way around the walls to provide a generous amount of easily accessible storage space. The drawers can be pulled all the way out, much like those of a filing cabinet, which means that the back of each drawer is easy to reach. As the top of the cabinets are reinforced, they can be used as seating, except where the record player is situated underneath the one overhead storage unit. The cabinets and drawers to each side of the turntable are used to house an extensive music collection, while the overhead storage unit houses books. A slim shelf, which is invisibly fixed so that it appears to "float," is fitted underneath the storage unit directly above the music collection. This is used to store stereo equipment within easy reach of those looking through the music drawers beneath. All of the storage units in this room are painted white to match the walls, which means that, when closed, they can "disappear" into the space, leaving only the turntable and stereo system visible.

space-saving
ideas

Door-frame Shelves

Overhead storage for a large collection of books

The owners of this house needed to store a vast library, without having the luxury of a dedicated space. Their solution is an ingenious use of space, with floor-to-ceiling shelves around the walls (including the corridors) and shelving that is recessed into the door frame. A shelf is also fitted above the door for books that need to be kept but do not need to be accessed frequently.

Cube Seat

This cube has a removable top, making it a seat with hidden storage

Inspired by the traditional piano stool, this upholstered cube can provide occasional seating and will act as the perfect side table for a living area. Additionally, the top can be removed to expose a hollow interior, where books and other items can be stored. For details on how to make this three-in-one storage solution, see Building a Cube, p. 98.

ways with shadow squares

2

Shadow squares are so called because they render objects in silhouette. Since they can take many shapes and be made in a number of variations, they can stylishly meet both storage and display requirements.

Shadow Table

Made from ply for extra strength, this would also be a perfect bedside table.

½ in. (12 mm.) birch ply, cut to size
   (see Project Dimensions, p. 96)
basic tool kit (see p. 88)
varnish and brush

1 Assemble your square, piece by piece, and glue it together (see Building a Shadow Square, steps 1–2, p. 97).

2 Apply bar clamps (see Clamping, p. 90) and keep them on overnight to ensure strong joints.

3 Sand as necessary and then wipe down with a clean cloth.

4 Apply varnish and leave to dry.

Shadow Shelf

Make to suit the dimensions of your objects or the size of the room.

¾ in. (18 mm.) mdf, cut to size (see Project Dimensions, p. 96)
basic tool kit (see p. 88)
latex flat or eggshell paint
batten and fixings (see Shelf Supports, p. 93)

1 Assemble your shelf and, using wood or polyurethane glue (see Gluing, p. 90), glue the four sides together (see Building a Shadow Square, steps 1–2, p. 97).

2 Using sash cramps (see Clamping, p. 90), hold the shelves in position so that you can screw them together for extra strength (see Building a Shadow Square, steps 3–4, p. 97).

3 Apply wood filler over the screw heads; leave to dry.

4 Sand the finished shelf, wipe down with a cloth, and then paint.

5 Cut the batten to the internal horizontal dimensions of the shelf.

6 Using a spirit level for positioning, screw the batten into place on the wall (see Shelf Supports, p. 93).

7 Paint the batten to match the shelf; leave to dry.

8 Push the shelf over the batten so that the top rests on the batten and the shelf is flush against the wall.

9 Screw the batten to the underside of the shelf top.

Who doesn't remember the pleading of long-suffering parents to "clean up your room" when, as adolescents, mess was a bid for freedom and self-expression. Older and wiser, we now recognize that a bedroom benefits from an atmosphere of tranquility and calm and that it is difficult to sleep surrounded by an unruly din of possessions. Waking up in a clutter-free environment starts the day on the right foot.

bedrooms

You may be fortunate enough to have walk-in closets in your bedroom, in which case any extra storage can be provided by chests of drawers and the like. But in an older house, the closet space may be inadequate. The easy solution here is an armoire. Attractive ones can often be found in antique stores and in flea markets. But these tend to be awkwardly shaped pieces of furniture, difficult to maneuver in and out of rooms. A far more efficient option is a built-in closet system, consisting of various units such as

1 Folding mirrored doors reflect light and space back into the room. These conceal not only hanging space but also shelving and drawers for smaller items of clothing, as well as bedding.

2 A cherished collection of vintage shoes is kept in a deep drawer to protect them from everyday dust and light but is easily accessible when the drawer is opened. A small rail within the drawer ensures that the shoes stand upright.

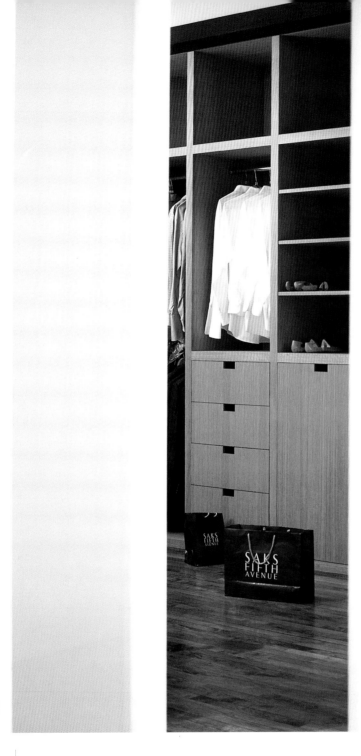

| recipes and ideas

hanging space, shelves, and drawers, with appropriate doors. You can select these from ready-made ranges and fit them yourself, or you can hire a carpenter to build a system for you. Such refinements as louvered or mirrored doors will make the system a visual as well as practical asset for the room.

Organize existing closet space efficiently to give yourself the right amount of hanging space for clothes that have to be hung (long and short), shelving for items that need to be folded such as T-shirts and knitwear, plus shoe racks and so on. If you are very time-poor (and relatively cash-rich) there are companies that will do this job for you. Smaller items, such as underwear, need smaller shelves or drawers, which can either be incorporated into a larger unit or bought as a stand-alone piece. If you are something of a shopaholic and your wardrobe is ever expanding, make yourself a rule (and stick to it) that each time you buy something new, something else has to go—into the trash, to charity, to a sister or friend—whatever.

There may be some proud possessions that you would rather look at than hide away—a vintage dress, antique kimono, or embroidered piano shawl, for example. Use it as decoration in a bedroom, hung onto the walls or over the bed. You could also hang up beautiful shopping bags or stack up shoe boxes to lend your room a boutique charm, while perfume bottles grouped on a bedside table can add instant decoration.

While a bedside table counts as an essential, a dressing table must be the ultimate indulgence—your own little

1 Here a spare room off the main bedroom has been given a new lease on life as a dressing room. Sliding doors lead through to an open area, with a closet fixed along one wall and fitted with drawers, shelves, closet and hanging space.

2 A contemporary take on the walk-in closet. To the left of the open doorway is a hanging rail for coats, shirts, and dresses, while the series of hollow box shelving on the back wall provides both decoration and storage for smaller items. Pairs of shoes are filed underneath the clothes rail.

shrine to beauty. It is so much more elegant to perch on an upholstered stool in front of a dressing table, its drawers full of all the secret ingredients of your toilette, than to sit on the bed or lean over the bathroom basin in clinical lighting. You can keep your underwear and cosmetics here and display photographs or treasured objects on the top, and if you like writing letters or keeping a diary, you could also use it as a desk. However, a dressing table does take up considerable space, so consider what else you need to fit into the room before you decide to live this particular dream.

The bedroom is a natural place for a laundry basket if you tend to undress here, rather than in the bathroom. If you like to watch television or listen to music while curled up under the covers, you will need to decide whether to fix the set or music system directly to the wall, find space on a larger piece of furniture, or buy a television/stereo cabinet, which will take up floor space.

Use any space under the bed to store things that aren't needed often, such as spare blankets and out-of-season clothing. Use a spare bedroom (if you have one) to keep large items that are needed only occasionally, from suitcases to skis. Avoid letting these take over the room; any guests

will have their own possessions. If you don't have a spare room, use the back of your tallest closet, or find unused space in the basement, utility room, or garage.

In a family house or apartment, there will be more than one bedroom to keep under control. The paraphernalia of a baby or infant is vast and specific, but try to resist investing too much in fun-size nursery furniture which won't grow with your child. If children are sharing and the space is large enough, try to make sure that each child has their own storage unit for clothing, toys, school materials, and books and a little extra space for their own little secrets.

1 Temporary extra storage space can be provided by a freestanding rail on casters like this one, which has a shelf below for shoes—a good solution for a closet-less guest room.

2 Different aesthetics suit different spaces. Here, clothes are stored within large woven baskets stacked on shelves; vintage dresses hang from the handles to hint at their contents.

3 A chest of drawers sits underneath a clothes rail to offer both hanging and folding storage. Whether positioned inside an existing fitted closet or in a large open space, doors fitted across the front ensure that everything is kept out of sight.

While younger children seem naturally to enjoy order (most of the time), there is little point in trying to impose boot-camp rules in an older child's bedroom. While they may be under your roof, this is their room—their domain— and they won't thank you for invasive clean-up visits. All you can do is lead by example and try to instill within them a respect for their environment and a responsibility for their own possessions.

In many ways your bedroom is the most important room in the house. When you retreat for the night, the last thing you want to see is discarded underwear on the floor or clean clothes spilling out of an over-full closet. In the morning you shouldn't have to face rifling through deep, dark drawers and piles of creased clothing to find the day's outfit. Keep it streamlined and simple—start with the closet and the rest will follow. Make room for yourself to dream.

1 This child's closet has been custom designed to store both clothes and toys and to provide an integral play area. When the sides of the wardrobe are pulled down, they become useful surfaces for play and, later in life, for homework. A suspended shelf is hung from the back wall.

2 When not in use, the shelf disappears into the background and the child's closet is closed to leave only an intriguing architectural feature—proving that high style and children can be bedfellows.

3 This complex closet system provides a rail for clothing, drawers for folded items, and a high shelf for accessories and boxes. A television has been built into the unit at a height that corresponds to the eye-level of the viewer in the low bed.

4 When the closet is closed, a door hiding the television set can be opened independently, making the screen a focal point with few visual distractions.

① Portrait of a room

This bedroom has been customized to provide a large amount
of storage in a relatively small space. The floor-to-ceiling closet
is fitted with a space-saving, double-hanging rail at one end for
shorter items of clothing. A hook on the wall next to the closet
is used to hang tomorrow's outfit to save time in the mornings.
A clothes basket underneath collects anything waiting to be
washed. Shoes are filed in open pigeonholes, fitted along
another wall, and the adjacent dressing-table unit provides
three further levels of storage.

Under-bed Drawers

*A bed rests on a platform into
which drawers are fitted*

If you have high ceilings, consider
building up to use vertical space,
particularly in a small room where
there is little other storage space
available. Here, the sleeping area is
set on a raised platform, which
separates the bed from the rest of
the bedroom. Deep drawers are
integrated into the platform to house
clothing and extra blankets—the
drawers can be pulled all the way out
for complete access to all of the
stored items. This efficient storage
ensures Zen-like calm in the
Japanese-influenced room.

Recessed Raised Bed

Open pigeonhole steps lead up to a raised bed, recessed into the wall

A bed needs little vertical space above it – just enough to someone to sit, which makes a raised bed a perfect way to make use of the vertical space in a room. In a child's bedroom it also provides a larger area underneath for playing, entertaining and studying. The head of the bed disappears into a recess which is taken up at floor level by cabinets. The steps up to this bed form a honeycomb of pigeonholes for the storage of toys and games.

Cabinet stairs

Lidded boxes, a closet and a cabinet are integrated into the steps

In this very small space, the raised bed is a huge benefit but it doesn't allow for any clothing storage around the bed as one would normally find in a bedroom. However, an innovative and extremely effective solution has been found. A full-size closet and cabinet have been integrated into the steps that lead up the platform. Additionally, the tread on each step can be lifted to reveal an individual storage box beneath. This combination offers a large amount of essential storage condensed into a tiny space.

Shelving unit room divide

A large, floor-standing shelving unit
divides a bedroom and bathroom

1 in. (24 mm.) plywood, cut to size
    (see Project Dimensions, p. 96)
basic tool kit (see p. 88)
³⁄₁₆ in. (4 mm.) hardboard
wood filler
varnish and brush

1 Glue the top, bottom and side
pieces of the unit at right angles and
screw them together for extra
strength using countersunk screws
(see Gluing and Screwing, p. 90).
Leave to dry.

2 Measure and mark the positions of
the horizontal shelves and then glue
and screw them onto the sides of the
unit. Leave until the glue is dry.

3 Measure and mark the positions of
each of the vertical dividers, and then
glue them into place. Leave to dry.

4 Decide how many shelves you
would like to leave open and how
many need to be fitted with the
hardboard backing. It will be easier to
fix one large piece of hardboard as a
backing for a number of the shelves
at one time. Cut the hardboard into
the required pieces and nail each
onto the back of the unit in the
appropriate positions.

5 Apply filler over the screwheads
and, when dry, sand as necessary.

6 Varnish the finished unit and leave
to dry before positioning in the room.

Perspex Clothing System

Modern and stylish, with clothing that
appears to be hanging in space

lengths of sheet and rod Perspex,
  pre-cut to suit your space (see
    Project Dimensions, p. 96)
basic tool kit (see p. 88)
paint to match the wall
silicone sealant

1 Measure and mark the wall where
the rod is to be fixed, and drill a
corresponding hole 2 in. (5 cm.)
deep to fit the width of the rod.

2 Paint the inside of the hole to
match the wall, and leave to dry.

3 Apply silicone sealant to the hole
and fix the length of Perspex rod
inside the hole, supporting the rod
until the silicone has set.

4 Apply a thin strip of silicone to the
top of each shelf support (see Shelf
Supports, p. 92) and press onto the
underside of the shelf.

5 Wipe off any excess silicone with a
damp finger. Support both pieces of
Perspex until the silicone has set.

6 Using masking tape, mark the top
line of the shelf on the wall.

7 Apply silicone to the back of the
shelf and shelf supports, and press
into position on the wall.

8 Make sure that the shelves are
level before the silicone sets.

9 Wipe off any excess silicone, and
support the shelf until set in position.

Often the smallest room in the house, the bathroom offers relatively little storage, especially considering that this is usually a shared space. A bathroom must work efficiently but, almost equally importantly, should also not feel too clinical or soulless, answering the very different needs of both the inevitable morning rush and the more indulgent evening bath by candlelight—aesthetics and practicality in harmony.

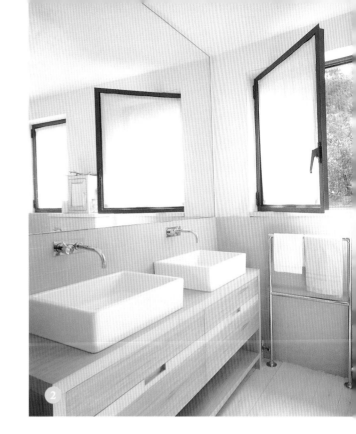

bathrooms

Here, as elsewhere, consider what needs to be on hand for day to day use, what should be stored away, and how far away to store it. Some bathroom products are decorative and can be kept on display, perhaps on open shelving or grouped in baskets around the room. A deep ledge along a wall above or close to the bathtub will keep everything from towels to toiletries conveniently within reach, while a small glass shelf fitted above the basin keeps the essentials close at hand while maximizing available light.

1 The storage is almost invisible in this bathroom, as it is hidden behind full-height closet doors that work on a push-catch mechanism. The basin is positioned behind the doors, along with grooming essentials, and can be hidden away so that the marble bathtub is the only focus.

2 If there is enough space, two basins in a shared bathroom are an unusually practical indulgence. Cosmetics and wash kits lie in the closed drawers beneath, while towels are both dried and stored on a towel-warming rail.

Other bathroom items are better hidden away out of sight. The interiors of built-in cabinets can be customized to enable bulky items to be stored along with smaller items. Freestanding units provide a flexible solution for things that you want kept concealed and dry, since they can be positioned at the most useful location within the room. Wall-hung cabinets are another good option, particularly if they can be locked to keep cleaning products and medicines out of the reach of children, while a cabinet with a mirrored front makes a separate mirror unnecessary. Other wall-mounted fittings, such as toothbrush holders and soap dishes, help to keep the basin clutter free, while showers can be fitted with racks for soaps, sponges, and shampoos.

The plumbing usually determines the basic plan of a bathroom, leaving little flexibility in the overall design. If you are renovating a small bathroom, consider concealing the tank and plumbing behind a false wall fitted with concealed cabinets or recessed niches. The loss of floor space is more than outweighed by the gain of more storage, with the added benefit that any ugly pipework is hidden to give a more streamlined look to the whole room. Modernists may want to build cabinets around the base of toilet and basin, which will create more usable space.

Piles of clean, soft towels within easy reach of the bathtub or shower are a must in any bathroom. A towel-warming rail—very popular in Europe—adds a touch of luxury. If you have an attractive collection of fluffy towels

① In this upscale bathroom, with Philippe Starck-designed bathtub and basin, the towels are stored along and below a low bench seat, while all other surfaces are kept clean and clutter free.

② In this seaside bathroom, a mirror-fronted unit sits on a shelf alongside reclaimed glass containers holding small items such as cotton balls, hair accessories, and votive candles. A combined towel rail and clothes hook is reflected in the mirror.

③ Here robes are hung within a storage unit, which has a shelf for towels above. The glass shelf underneath the mirror provides a convenient surface for soaps and cosmetics.

and washcloths in coordinated colors, display them on open shelves; those that are somewhat old and mismatched are best concealed in a cabinet. If floor space is tight, make use of wall space, and fix a towel rack above the bathtub or hooks to the back of the door. In a small bathroom, at least everything is close at hand.

If you have a larger bathroom, think about adding a chair, for removed clothes, or a stool with a removable lid which provides extra storage within. But whatever the size of your room, don't make functionality your only concern. Traditionally, the bathroom plays an important role as a sanctuary. It should not be diminished by pure, mechanical functionalism, but should appeal directly to the senses.

1 The ultimate in streamlining, a series of cabinets built into this wall conceal day-to-day items and ensure that nothing but the architecture is ever on display. The hinged cabinet fronts can be pulled to horizontal to provide useful work surfaces, while the mirrored wall at right creates an illusion of unending space.

2 The clean lines of this calm, rather Zen-like space are echoed in the custom-made wooden bench with integral storage, which also acts as a shelf. Extra storage is hidden behind mirrored doors and supplemented by a large basket for daily laundry.

Towel Store

*Dark wooden pigeonholes make
unusual storage for rolled towels*

Towels take up a lot of storage
space, particularly when a large family
has to share the bathroom and fresh
towels are always needed close at
hand. Here, every freshly laundered
towel has been rolled tightly to take
up the smallest amount of space
possible. The wall of open
pigeonholes provides excellent easy-
to-access storage for the towels,
along with other small items such as
cosmetics and toiletries, and has
become an interesting design feature
in its own right.

Above-tank Shelving

Shelving recessed over the tank to provide accessible storage

In a tiny room, the only way to go is up. Here, in a long, narrow bathroom, the space over the water tank has been opened up to provide four sturdy shelves and the tank itself has been covered over to make a closed cabinet to one side. As the shelves are open to view, everything has been stored away in boxes of various sizes, except the freshly laundered towels which are stacked directly onto the shelf for easy access.

Under-sink Baskets

Brightly colored baskets sit underneath a wooden drawer unit

In this contemporary bathroom, the basin is fitted into a wall-to-wall worktop. Drawers integrated into the worktop are lockable, so that medicines can be kept out of the reach of inquisitive children. On the shelf underneath the unit sit a row of natural, handwoven baskets, which are being used to store toiletries and cosmetics, as well as hair accessories and jewelry. Underneath these are another row of shallower baskets, used to store towels.

Bath Shelf

This runs from wall to wall for easy access to bathing essentials.

½ in. (12 mm.) mdf, cut to size (see
   Project Dimensions, p. 96)
latex flat paint or bathroom paint
basic tool kit (see p. 88)
wide paintbrush
batten and hardware (see p. 93)

1 Glue the facia trim onto the edges of both the top and bottom pieces of the shelf, so that you have a deep "C" shape that is open along the sides and back.

2 Using countersinking screws for invisible construction, screw the facia trim into place from the front (see Screwing, p. 90).

3 Apply filler over the screwheads, and leave to dry.

4 Lightly sand the finished shelf, and then wipe with a clean cloth.

5 Apply two coats of paint to the shelf; leave to dry.

6 Measure and mark the position of the shelf on the wall.

7 Cut the batten to the length of the internal dimensions of the shelf, and screw into position on the wall.

8 Push the shelf over the batten so that it is flush against the wall and screw batten and shelf together from underneath (see Shelf Supports, p. 93).

Shelves with Terry Cloth Curtains

A perfect fabric for bathrooms, terry cloth is easy to launder.

chrome shelving unit (see Note)
terry cloth
length of cane or dowel
basic tool kit (see p. 88)

1 Retaining a small piece for the ties, cut the terry cloth into four lengths which will, when hemmed, fit the two sides and front of your unit.

2 Hem the edges of each length of terry cloth, leaving enough space in the two front panels to run a cane or dowel through the hem at the top as a runner along the front of the unit.

3 With the remaining terry cloth, make pairs of ties to attach each corner of each panel to the top of the shelving unit.

4 Using a needle and thread to match the terry cloth, sew the ties to the panels.

5 Tie the side panels onto the unit.

6 Thread the dowel or cane through the top hem of the two front panels to keep them rigid and level, and tie the panels onto the unit.

Note: We used a purchased chrome shelving unit, but you could use any unused unit that you have in your home already. If you can't tie your panels on, attach runners on the top and tie the material onto these.

The kitchen remains the heart of the modern home—not simply a functional area where food is stored, prepared and cooked, but also a social space where family members eat together, talk on the phone, finish homework, and entertain friends. Ergonomics should be tempered with atmosphere to ensure that the kitchen not only works well but also remains an appealing room in which to spend time.

kitchens

House plans of the past reveal that vast areas were once dedicated to kitchens, especially those of well-to-do households who kept a cook and an invariably well-stocked larder. Over the past one hundred years, kitchens—at least the area given over to its machinery and storage—have shrunk more dramatically than any other room in the house. There are a number of explanations for this downsizing: food no longer tends to be prepared so completely from scratch, and the machinery of cooking and washing has

1 There is something very attractive about the apparent honesty of this kitchen. All foodstuffs and utensils are open to the room on modular shelving, built around a central fireplace, which means that nothing is ever buried away and forgotten. The overall effect is quirky and individual.

2 Here a fitted kitchen has been supplemented by open shelving. Edit possessions down to what is beautiful and useful and you won't need to hide anything away.

1. A large island unit can almost double surface and storage space. In this modern kitchen, the base of the unit is divided into open pigeonholes, which are filled with the more beautiful everyday items. The best island units are not fixed to the floor but run on casters, which means that they are flexible enough to wheel out of the way when not required.

2. On the kitchen side of the fixed island are the appliances and sink; on the other, and close to the table, sliding doors conceal all eating utensils. These sliding doors are echoed on the back wall of the kitchen, where they are used to conceal shelving.

3. Ergonomics and practicality are not the only considerations. Here the kitchen has been designed to show off the beauty of the items stored within: the ceramics stacked behind the glass become part of the decoration; pretty lanterns hanging from the ceiling underline this aesthetic approach.

become more compact. With the introduction of the fitted kitchen, now so prevalent in the contemporary home, things have become even more streamlined.

A well-planned, fitted kitchen should answer all of your storage needs, providing enough organized space for food and drink, dishes, utensils, pots, and pans. It may also include space for extra high-tech, labor-saving gadgetry, from blenders and food processors to ice-cream machines and microwaves, and the miscellaneous items that always seem to end up in the kitchen, such as candles, batteries, and matches.

It makes sense to site your larger appliances—the washing machine and tumble dryer and, of course, the increasingly indispensable dishwasher—within an overall fitted kitchen, which will often include spaces for them to be installed. To save extra space and give yourself more storage room in a fitted kitchen, buy an integrated washer-dryer. In a small house or open-plan apartment, choose the quietest models available, so that you can run them at night and still get to sleep. Your plumbing will dictate, to an extent at

① Portrait of a room

This light, airy kitchen is also used as a work space, which creates even more pressure on the available space. The solution found here combines different elements. A majority of closed storage keeps most things hidden away when not required. One open pigeonhole above the oven gives easy access to the most regularly used food. The kitchen worktop has been customized to become a desk and the theme of open and closed storage is continued. Finished projects are stored away in the top cupboard, with on-going projects and stationery stored in glass-fronted cabinets just above the desk. Open shelves hold both work and cookery books.

least, where these can be located; and most dryers need to be positioned by an outside wall, to accommodate the exhaust vent. Remember to take note of the measurements of the spaces you have for these appliances—models (and kitchen units) vary in size, and you don't want to spend a significant amount of money on something that doesn't fit in the space available.

If your kitchen is exposed to your living or dining area, think about creating a closed-off utility area for storing the noisier appliances, such as the washer, dryer, or dishwasher. If restrictions of space rule this out, perhaps you could consider fitting sliding doors to screen off the kitchen when entertaining. If you do manage to get an area of the kitchen behind a door or screen, perhaps you could also use this space to store your recycling boxes or bulk-bought items, such as detergent.

As a rule, unfitted kitchens require more space and are less efficient than fitted, while closed cabinets are generally more useful than open shelves, since they are more effective at protecting possessions from cooking spatters and water splashes. In reality, most kitchens contain a combination of fitted and unfitted storage, including both open and closed. This gives a degree of flexibility when organizing your kitchen and allows less attractive items to be hidden away while any beautifully packaged food and well-designed glassware can remain on view.

Open shelving holds cook books and food that is often used.

Frosted glass-fronted cabinets allow items inside to be semi-visible.

Below-counter shelving has solid doors to hide the pots and pans from sight.

A part of the work surface has been lowered and widened for use as a desk.

If the reality of your kitchen falls somewhat short of the dream, there are lots of things that you can do to improve the efficiency of what already exists, from customizing cabinet interiors to putting up new shelving or utensil racks. If you have the space, you could also invest in a piece of freestanding furniture, such as a dresser or serving cart, which can offer both storage space and extra work surfaces. Lighten the load through regular spring-cleanings, junking anything, equipment or food, that hasn't seen the light of day for the past year. The more frequently you shop, the less storage space you will need for food.

As in other rooms, decide which items need to be most accessible and which are used less regularly, as this will affect how things are best stored within the space. For ease of use, try to position china cabinets and utensil drawers close to the dishwasher or sink, and the essential groceries, such as oils and spices, within two steps of the range.

Floor-to-ceiling units provide lots of storage where the turkey-roasting pan or punch bowl can be stored in out-of-the-way overhead places, while the day-to-day items are easy to reach. If your kitchen is large, you may use it for other activities, which themselves require tools or equipment that will need to be stored, so make sure that you are using all available room. Shelves or drawers on fully extendible runners maximize existing space and should put an end to rummaging around in the back of dark cupboards.

With any kitchen larger than a galley kitchen, it makes sense to give yourself the option of eating in the kitchen. In a relatively small space choose a table with a fold-down leaf, which can be stowed back against the wall when not in use to maximize circulation space. Instead of chairs, choose long, low benches that can be stored under the table between meals. For a very small space there are tables that fold right back to the wall, but whatever the size of your table, it could easily double up as a work surface for household paperwork. The frame of the table could be fitted with a couple of drawers or shelves for utensils, take-out menus and the like.

A breakfast bar may sound horribly '70s but is actually a clever way to save space, while still providing a comfortable place to sit and eat. If your kitchen has a central island, then raise up a portion of the work surface—make sure that it does not interrupt the working triangle of sink, oven, and refrigerator—and line up a couple of stools in front of it.

As in the rest of the house, remember to exploit the storage potential provided by vertical surfaces. Run shelves all the way along any otherwise uninterrupted walls to store cook books, a knife block, or condiments. Hang pots and pans from the ceiling, around a central island or underneath high shelves or cabinets to use up less surface space.

A new kitchen is about the most expensive home improvement that you can make and probably the quickest way to add value to your home. If you are able to upgrade, put a lot of thought into the planning, particularly with regard to safety—you need to ensure a clear passage around the room so that carrying hot, heavy pans from the oven or cooktop to the sink is not hazardous. If you are using a specialist design company, be sure to brief them comprehensively as to how you work within the space and what your particular priorities are.

Cooking and eating should be stimulating, enjoyable activities and not complicated by messy, overloaded worktops, hard labor, and out-of-control cabinets. A streamlined kitchen that is hygienic, safe, and easy to clean, with well-planned storage for all your needs, will tempt you into culinary creativity.

1. The design of this kitchen has taken into account the fact that it is part of a larger space: when it is not being used, everything save the sink is concealed behind streamlined cabinet fronts.

2. The units here are used as a partition between the kitchen and dining areas of this open-plan space, which means that any cooking mess can be forgotten at least for the duration of the meal. Cabinets and drawers of different sizes offer an unusual look with a practical approach.

3. A pair of sliding doors seal off this small kitchen area when not in use. Fitted units provide the most efficient storage option for a small space.

space-saving ideas

Shallow Floor-to-ceiling Shelves

Everything in this narrow space is visible and accessible

In a narrow room, maximum use must be made of vertical space. Here, floor-to-ceiling shallow shelves allow all things to be stored where they can be seen and are easy to find. Glass jars are used to store all the cooking essentials, such as sugar, flour and rice, and help to regulate the look of the room. Beyond the shelves the range has been recessed into the wall so that nothing impinges on the narrow floor space in the room. Opposite the range, a slim unit houses the sink and is fitted with drawers and closed cabinets for pots, pans, china and utensils.

Pull-out Shelving

This ensures that you use the full depth of your cupboards

In such a tiny kitchen area, all the available storage space must be used. With pull-out, floor-to-ceiling cupboards that have internal shelving, the entire depth of the storage unit can be accessed with ease and so can be fully used at all times. On the opposite side of the kitchen, a narrow unit with fitted cupboards stores kitchen equipment and has an integrated breakfast bar on the top to allow for informal dining.

Under-counter Boxes

Simple and efficient, these boxes can be stored anywhere

These metallic boxes are made out of stainless steel so that they won't rust in the humidity of a kitchen, but plastic boxes would work just as effectively. Placed underneath a table or worktop they can be filled with any equipment or tools that you need to keep but just can't find a home for anywhere else.

Felt-covered Bulletin Board

Give each member of the family, or day of the week, their own square.

felt (treated for flame retardancy—
    see Fabric, p.89)
cork tiles
spray adhesive (see Note, below)
skeleton caulking plus cartridge

1 Cut felt to cover each cork tile so that it overlaps onto the back.

2 Using spray adhesive, attach the felt to the cork.

3 Glue each tile separately to the wall, butting each up to the next.

Note: Check that the spray adhesive will not adversely affect flame retardancy.

Magnetic Board

Custom-made to suit your space, with a tin can container attached.

silicone sealant (see Metal, p. 89)
empty, cleaned tin can
sheet metal, cut to size
    (see Metal, p. 89)
batten and hardware (see Shelf
    Supports, p. 93)

1 Using silicone sealant, attach a cleaned can to the front of the metal.

2 Cut a narrow batten to fit the depth available behind the metal board.

3 Screw the batten into position on the wall, apply silicone sealant and press the board onto it, so that the top edge rests on the batten and the board sits flush against the wall.

Pocket Board

Being waterproof, oilcloth is perfect both for kitchen utensils and recipes.

oilcloth (see Fabric, p. 89)
bulletin board (or any square board)
basic tool kit (see p. 88)

1 Cut the fabric to the size of the board, allowing a large hem at each side and an even larger hem at top and bottom so that the fabric can be tucked to form deep-enough pockets (see Note, below).

2 Staple the oilcloth to the top back of the board and, working down, fold it back over itself at two places equidistant down the board to form your pockets.

3 Staple at the sides of the pockets and then around the back of the board to secure the rest of the fabric.

Note: On our board, which measures 16 x 23 in. (41 x 58 cm.), we added 4 in. (10 cm.) extra on each side of the board and 18 in. (45 cm.) extra at top and bottom to form the pockets.

ways to clutter-free counters

A work space is now a fact of life in many homes: as an office for the self-employed professional, as an area dedicated to life's paperwork, or as anything between the two. This does not necessarily mean sacrificing a whole room to hard-edged gadgets and style-free furniture. Remember to include a few user-friendly textures. People work better when they are happier, and, after all, this is still your home.

work spaces

When did the "den" become the home office? It may have been as computers were welcomed into the home and women gained ground in this traditionally masculine domain. Gone are the dark wood and "men's club" leather chairs, in favor of lighter, brighter, more ergonomic and democratic furnishings.

Depending on the size of the house and the nature of the labor, a work space can range from a dedicated studio to an area within a room that also has to serve quite another

1 This shared work space can be separated from the living area by a pair of space-saving folding doors. The office is arranged against a wall and comprises a long desk below a wall of shelving to the ceiling, open for easy reference. The less often a document is used the farther away from the desk it is filed.

2 This is about as basic as filing systems come—but it works for the owner. Storage is effective only if it meets your needs.

1 This individual space makes a feature of tools and equipment, which are displayed in pigeon-holes on open shelving. This is a system that proves practical as well as decorative, since everything is always on view to the user and doesn't have to be hunted down. Pictures are displayed in a row around the perimeter of the room to stimulate creativity.

2 Offices aren't always defined by filing cabinets. File-sized shelving attached to a wall above a desk makes for paperwork that is contained, yet easy to reach.

purpose (for example a dining room or little-used guest room furnished with a sofa bed or Murphy bed). It can even take the form of a single self-contained unit or piece of furniture.

To assess storage requirements here, begin by itemizing the equipment that you use: different professions have very different paraphernalia. Technology makes its own demands on space, and most 21st-century home offices need at least a computer, fax, and phone, while some call for other more career-specific equipment, from a sewing machine to a drawing board or color printer. If you do use electronic equipment, remember to make sure that you have enough

outlets, so that you can position it, and task lighting, where you want them.

Until the paperless office truly becomes reality (if indeed it ever will), most home office storage will probably be taken up with filing projects, past and present. Lighten the load by sifting through files periodically, chucking out anything of dubious value that the I.R.S. does not require you to keep. You may not want to opt for obviously office-like storage solutions for paperwork. There is no reason for the gray and beige of the corporate office to infiltrate the home. Working environments don't have to be wipe-clean

and anonymous. It should be easier to work here, where you are at your most comfortable, than in a rabbit-hutch workstation of oppressive uniformity, on a floor shared by others. A home office should reflect your individuality, as should the storage.

While expanding files and filing cabinets can look great in an apartment with an industrial aesthetic, they may look out of keeping if your style is more traditional than modern. It is possible to customize more domestic shapes and finishes to keep the office in step with the rest of the home. You don't need a mobile computer stand to house a computer, especially if you use a laptop—a dining table will do, although you should make sure that you have an ergonomic chair on which to sit. Beauty and utility should go hand in hand.

If you have to hold meetings in your home office, you will need to make doubly sure that your space looks passably professional. It is also a good idea to locate your office close to the entrance to your home, so that clients and colleagues won't have to traipse through the whole house to get there.

In a small or dual-purpose space, good storage is crucial and neatness almost forced upon you, or work will creep out of its allocated space and invade the rest of the house. Careful planning is particularly important in a multi-functional space in order for it to fulfill, not fail, both roles. Partition off a corner of the room to divide it into zones, or choose freestanding storage on casters which can be wheeled away out of "office hours." In a small space, choose wall-mounted shelves, which take up less space than free-standing units—a built-in or modular shelving system may be the most useful answer.

Efficient home office storage is for those with a healthy horror of, not an unhealthy interest in, filing. Try to maintain a clean-desk policy by putting away everything that is no longer needed. Keeping everything off the primary work surface apart from the task immediately in hand has been shown to improve concentration by minimizing visual distractions. Mess equals visual noise. It is difficult to concentrate or be creative in chaos.

A huge, freestanding cabinet on casters provides large amounts of storage in this photographer's studio and home. The fact that it is on wheels means that it can be pushed away from the window and up against a wall, when natural light is required, and pulled out only to access the shelves on one side.

This inexpensive shelving is filled with boxes dedicated to different projects and materials. Little-used items are kept at the top, frequently referenced materials at waist and eye level.

Cabinet Work Space

A pull-out work station is stored
behind sliding doors

Behind the sliding doors of this
narrow room is a small home office.
The desk has a pull-out extension,
seen here as a shelf underneath, to
make the working area bigger – a
keyboard is permanently stored here
as it can be pushed out of sight
when the extension is not needed.
The stool fits neatly underneath the
desk when it is not in use. The desk
itself fits beneath three broad, deep
shelves on which sit baskets full of
projects past and present, stationery
and reference materials.

Table-leg Filing Cabinet

Easy organization and speedy filing for a small work area

This desk is supported by a pair of filing cabinets with shallow drawers so that paperwork is filed without the worker even having to move from their chair. This is a simple and effective solution that is relatively inexpensive to do. The top of the desk needs to be of a material sturdy enough to support the weight of your work essentials.

Shelf and Drawer Wall

Back-to-back shelving and deep drawers to use dead space

The most has been made of this unusual space. Drawers have been built into the side of a bookcase to make use of both faces of the wall. The floor-to-ceiling bookshelves are built into the wall next to the door and ensure that every research journal and book is within easy reach. The drawers are very deep to make use of all the space that would otherwise be inaccessible. The two shelves above are recessed into the corner again to make use of every inch of storage space.

Desk Shelving

An entire home office, made to measure, with a wider shelf as a desk.

¾ in. (18 mm.) and ¾ in. (12 mm.) mdf, cut to size (see Project Dimensions, p. 96)

basic tool kit (see p. 88)

eggshell or gloss paint

lengths of dowel or batten and hardware (see Shelf Supports, p. 93)

1 Make the desk and shelves, by gluing and screwing each facia trim to the outside edges of the appropriate pieces of mdf (see Gluing and Screwing, p. 90).

2 Using fine-grade sandpaper, sand all the faces of the desk and shelves that will be exposed; wipe clean.

3 Paint the desk and shelves with at least two coats of paint; leave to dry.

4 Measure and mark the positions of the desk and shelves on the wall, making sure they will be level.

5 Using the interior batten method (see Shelf Supports, p. 93) and a spirit level, fix the desk and shelves to the wall.

Note: If the desk or shelves will need to take a lot of weight, use additional shelf supports (see p. 93) as well as the batten method. Screw the extra supports underneath the desk and shelves at suitable intervals, then fix them to the wall.

ways
to a clean
desk

Customized Boxes

Simple and graphic, this uses a suitable storage box for each stationery item.

purchased cardboard or reinforced
  paper boxes
personal collage materials
appropriate glue or glue gun

1 Choose an appropriate size and shape of box for each of the items you wish to store.

2 Using a glue gun or other glue appropriate to your material (see Working Materials, p. 88), attach a visual indicator of what is to be stored in each box onto the front edge, and leave to dry.

Note: These boxes can be bought inexpensively from stationery and department stores (see Suppliers, p. 100) but you could also easily utilize any old boxes (such as shoe boxes) that you have in your home. Use them on open shelving to hold a variety of objects, from pencils to photographs.

Painted Clip Board

An easy and effective way of
organizing your work week.

low-tack masking tape
2 paintbrushes (one very fine)
matte or eggshell paint in two
    contrasting colors
5 screw-in chrome hooks
number stencils
5 bulldog clips

1 Using masking tape, mask out a
rectangle on the wall to the required
size, overlapping the tape at the
corners.

2 Paint the rectangle with two coats
of your chosen paint, and leave to
dry before removing the masking
tape.

3 Measure five points equidistant
across the rectangle, about 4 in.
(10 cm.) from the top, and insert a
hook at each.

4 Stencil one number above each of
the hooks, from one to five, and
carefully paint these in with your
contrasting color.

5 Hang a bulldog clip from each hook
and use to store receipts, lists, or
daily schedules.

Pigeonholes

A unit that gives ample storage for office essentials (and luxuries).

¾ in. (18 mm.) mdf, cut to size (see
   Project Dimensions, p. 96)
basic tool kit (see p. 88)
eggshell or latex paint
batten and hardware (see Shelf
   Supports, p. 93)
2 large picture hangers (see p. 94)

1 Glue the top, bottom, and side pieces of the unit at right angles to the edges of the backboard and, for extra strength, screw them in from the back (see Gluing, Clamping, and Screwing, p. 90); leave to dry.

2 Measure and mark the positions of the horizontal shelves, and then glue and screw them onto the backboard as before. Leave until the glue is dry.

3 Measure and mark the positions of the dividers, and then glue and screw (or nail) in place; leave to dry.

4 Paint the unit and leave to dry.

5 Cut the batten to the same width as the pigeonhole unit, paint it to match and leave to dry.

6 Measure and mark a position for the batten on the wall; since this supports the unit, it needs to be at a suitable height above the desk. Screw in place.

7 Attach two large picture hangers to the top of the backboard, and screw the unit in place on the wall.

8 Screw the batten to the base of the unit from underneath.

If your house is built along traditional lines, you may well have areas with storage possibilities that have been overlooked and have the potential to ease the pressure on living, eating, and sleeping areas. In-between spaces such as halls, corridors, and even stairs can yield significant storage opportunities. And if you have an attic or basement, or even both, then these, too, can house overflow.

halls & corridors

Hallways mark the transition between public and private spaces and give visitors their first impressions of your home. It is all too easy to use these areas as a general dumping ground for outdoor clothing, dry cleaning, sports equipment, and so on.

Halls and corridors are areas of high traffic, their primary function being to keep the separate areas of the house connected, so it is important not to do anything that might disturb flow. Having said that, you should be able to

A modern space with an enviably large entrance hall. Built-in open shelving, with a wider under-shelf for use as a desk, has been constructed along the length of one wall, still leaving ample room for circulation. The area around the door stores outdoor equipment and clothing out of the way.

A series of small wooden boxes positioned by the front door is an inventive solution for small items; the keys in this house should rarely get lost.

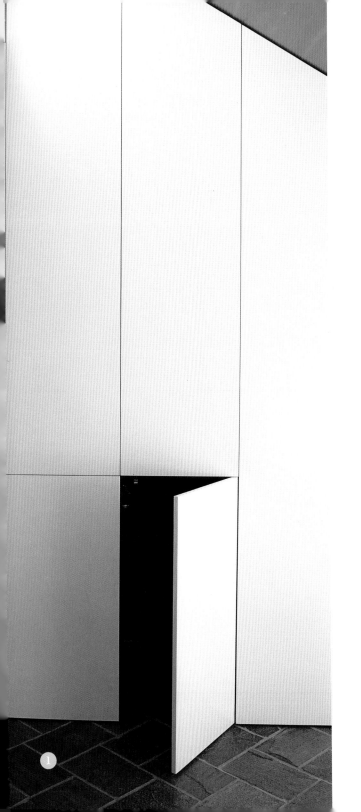

carve out enough space for a built-in closet that is at least big enough for coats, bags, and umbrellas. In a narrow hall, the slimline option is a row of hooks or pegs. If there is room for a console table by the door, then this will provide a natural resting place for the mail, keys, and small change. Perhaps you could hang a mirror above the table to create a focal point and a final place for you to check your lipstick or tie before heading out the door.

Exploit under-stair spaces by fitting closet doors, and create the perfect place to stash the vacuum-cleaner; you might even have room left above for a few shelves. Be resourceful: for example, on the landing of a two-flight staircase fit a bench seat with a fold-up lid, which has a secret life as a chest.

A waterproof basement or insulated attic is the perfect place to store items that are used infrequently, such as tools and sports equipment. Resist the temptation to dump everything into the room without organizing it first—your space will work harder if you plan it well. For a simple, inexpensive, solution, fit the room with a freestanding shelving system to provide for items of different scale.

There is a lot of potential for display in these ancillary spaces. The large wall areas provided by corridors are ideal for hanging photographs or canvases, while ceramics can be kept on shelves fitted within alcoves and niches.

In the modern home, where rooms often open directly onto one another, there are fewer storage opportunities although, as life becomes more informal and technology streamlined, we also—in theory—have less to store. Gone are the days of hats and coats; the contemporary family wears outdoor clothing that can easily be stashed in the bedroom (unless wet). Neither is there any need to find a home for the telephone as cordless models (with pre-programmed address books) are instead carried from room to room.

If you don't have the luxury of any transitional spaces in your home, nor a purpose-built utility room, you may be able to steal a corner of a garage for household overflow instead. Be ingenious and take as your mantra "There is no such thing as dead space."

1. It can be worth creating false walls and reducing room size to increase storage. A pair of large cabinets, for umbrellas, coats, sporting equipment, and the like, have been fitted into this false wall without compromising the architecture.

2. If you are short on horizontal space but have high ceilings, you can always build upward. The bed in this tiny apartment is elevated, with shelf units tucked in under the stairs. When not required, the shelves are concealed by hinged doors.

3. A serious shoe-aholic combines display with storage by utilizing the dead space along a stairwell. The unpainted area, once covered by carpet, demarcates a sufficiently wide passageway for those moving up and down the stairs.

Corridor Work Space

A work space with suitable storage in a specially designed wide corridor

Working from home can create problems of space, particularly when large quantities of plans or drawings need to be stored. In this home, a wide corridor has a second use as an area where work is both undertaken and stored. The plan-chest-style drawers that are fitted all along the wall protect on-going and finished projects, and the top of the drawers is well lit so that it can be used as a support for a drawing board. The open shelves above the drawers serve as storage for reference material.

Above-door Library

A bookshelf is hidden above a doorway to use vertical space

A lowered ceiling has been opened up in this tiny alcove vestibule to provide an unusual, elliptical storage shelf for books. As the books will be quite difficult to reach it suggests that they do not need to be read or referred to with any regularity, but are still titles that the owner would prefer not to throw out. Visitors to the apartment would not necessarily notice the feature so the space remains streamlined and calm.

Under-stair Wine Cellar

A striking feature that offers excellent customized storage for bottles

Small spaces can require careful planning in order to maximize storage. The solution that is chosen depends on what needs to be stored and in which locality in the home. The risers in this staircase, which leads off a kitchen and dining area, have been custom-designed to hold a growing wine collection. The collection can expand quite considerably before this storage space will be full.

Sliding Screen

A transparent screen creates storage,
even where there is little space

twinwall plastic (see Note, below)
lengths of aluminum track (see
  Using Track, p. 95)
coat hooks and hardware
basic tool kit (see p. 88)

1 Decide on the height and width of the screen and order the plastic cut to size, or cut it yourself with a fine-tooth saw (see Plastics, p. 89).

2 Have the track cut to fit, or cut it yourself with a hacksaw.

3 Unless you are using pre-drilled track, drill holes at regular intervals along the floor and ceiling track.

4 Using a suitable countersink bit, cut a recess in the track for the screw heads. The screws must be flush with the track for the screen to slide smoothly into the mountings.

5 Screw the track to the floor and ceiling with countersinking screws, and slide in the screen to fit.

6 Fix the hooks to the wall behind the screen.

Note: Twinwall plastic is available in different thicknesses and degrees of opacity—just choose the one that works best in your space.

3

practicalities

PLANNING AHEAD

This section tells you all you need to know about individual techniques for making the projects, and gives additional information for many of the ideas found in this book. You may have to adapt the dimensions to suit your space and your requirements, so always double-check your measurements before buying and working on your materials. If you are planning to fix your chosen project to a wall, check the material of the wall to ascertain the weight that it will be able to bear. Tap the wall with your knuckles; if you hear a dull thudding sound, the wall is likely to be hollow and therefore not a load-bearing wall. This means that you will have to be careful how much weight you put onto it. Also, double-check where the electric outlets and cables are positioned so that you don't drill through anything and cause yourself further problems.

When making any of the projects, do make sure that you are using materials that can be combined—find out which types of paint, glue, and varnish will work best with your materials and each other. Always be aware of your safety and if sawing or using chemical-based products, wear a face mask and work outside if possible.

BASIC TOOL KIT This is the basic tool kit that you will find useful when doing any of the projects and these items are therefore not listed for individual projects. See the project instructions for other more specific tools and materials.

Clamps	Pencil
Electric drill and	Sandpaper of various grades
countersink bit	Scissors
Glue gun	Screwdriver
Hacksaw or Jigsaw (with a	Screws of various sizes (with
few blades of different	wall plugs)
widths)	Sewing machine or
Hammer	needle/thread
Masking tape	Spirit level
Metal ruler	Staple gun
Nails of various sizes	Tape measure
Paintbrushes of various sizes	Wood glue

WORKING MATERIALS
Wood

If you want to use wood, do think about which kind of wood will work best for your project and consider the work that you will need to do to prepare it for use. Do not buy warped wood, as it will be difficult to work with—look along its length to check if it is twisted or warped. Wood is available either sawn or planed. Sawn wood looks slightly rougher in appearance but will be closer to the thickness that you requested, whereas planed wood is much smoother but may come up to ³⁄₁₆ in. (5 mm.) thinner than the measurement you wanted. For most of the projects, planed wood will be better as it gives a much smoother finish.

Boards are made mechanically from wood and are relatively inexpensive. They are also available in large sheets of approx. 2 yd. 17½ in. x 1 yd. 8¾ in. Go to your local hardware store to check the advantages and disadvantages of the various kinds before deciding which you need. We have used plywood for the Shadow Table (see Living Rooms, p. 28) and for the Shelving Unit Room-Divide (see Bedrooms, p. 42). Ply is made by gluing thin wood veneers in layers, with each layer at right angles to its neighbors, which means that the board is very strong and that there is little chance of warping. All wood can easily be cut to size at home if you have the right space and tools. If you buy your wood in planks from a woodyard, you shouldn't have to worry about the grain since planks are cut along the grain, although do take care when sawing through wood to make sure that it doesn't splinter on the underside of the cut.

When you are using countersunk screws and need to apply filler over the screwheads to give a flush finish, always use a proprietary wood filler as this will be relatively invisible. When sanding, always start with medium-grade sandpaper and finish with fine, and remember to only sand in line with the grain so that you don't scratch the surface. If you want to apply varnish or wax, these can be applied with a brush or a soft cloth. You may have to use two coats to get the right result. Different waxes and varnishes do give different finishes so double-check what you need.

Mdf (medium-density fiberboard)

This is a general-purpose building board (which is also known as particleboard) made from a highly compressed mixture of wood and other fibers. It is inert and therefore it won't shrink or warp, and is available in thicknesses ranging from ¼ in. (6 mm.) to 1⅜ in. (35 mm.). As it is so compressed it does not splinter when cut and leaves a clean edge—making sanding or finishing unnecessary. It can, however, be dangerous to cut particleboard yourself, as minute particles are released into the air. We recommend that you take your measurements with you when buying mdf and ask the DIY store to cut it to size for you. If you do want to do this work yourself, work outside where there is good air circulation and always wear a face mask and eye protection. Painting works particularly well on particleboard and a very good finish can be obtained, even on the edges, when no sanding has taken place.

Metal

As with mdf, we recommend that you take your measurements with you when buying metal and ask the DIY or hardware store to cut it for you. If you want to do this work yourself, use a hacksaw or a jigsaw with a metal blade, work outside and always wear gloves and protective eyewear. It is also recommended that you get the edges of the metal bent over so that you avoid sharp corners. Silicone is a perfect adhesive for metal and can be used directly on the wall. For the Magnetic Board (see Kitchens, p. 64) we use silicone to glue a sheet of metal to a batten (see Fixings, see p.93), which is fixed to the wall.

For the Magnetic Board (see Kitchens, p. 64) the sheet metal needs to be cut to size and the edges bent over before you can start work. The bent edges will create a very shallow hollow behind the sheet of metal. A batten to the same depth as the shallow hollow is screwed to the wall at the correct height. Silicone is applied to the batten and the board is then pushed over it, so that the top lip of the board is directly on top of the batten, and the edges of the board are flush against the wall.

Plastic

Plastic can be bought in widths of ½ in.–1 in. in a huge variety of types. We used Twinwall for the Sliding Screen (see Halls, p. 84) because it is strong but very light. We recommend that you have your plastic cut to size for you, because it is an expensive material and can be difficult to cut, but if you want to do this yourself you will need a fine-tooth saw. Two-pack glue works best for attaching plastic to plastic in an instant, but other adhesives are necessary when gluing plastic to a wall or another material. We used silicone for our Perspex Clothing System (see Bedrooms, p. 43) because it allows for some repositioning before it dries. Do remember, however, that when using silicone the glued item will need to be braced until the silicone has set it into position.

Fabric

When selecting a fabric, bear in mind that not all fabric is suitable for upholstery. It is important to take note of the manufacturers information displayed on the fabric. Upholstery fabric will have a high rub-test, which is an indication of how hardwearing it will be. In general, the thicker the fabric and the tighter the weave, the longer it will last. Even more importantly, when choosing a fabric you need to be aware of its flame retardancy (FR) rating. FR fabric has been treated with a chemical fire-retardant, but the effectiveness of this treatment can be affected by washing or by the use of spray adhesives. If your fabric is not FR then it must be used with an FR lining. It is often a wise step to treat fabric with a suitable stain resistor.

Choose a fabric that will work well with both your project and your interior. We used felt for the Cube Seat (see Living Rooms, p. 27) and the Felt-covered Pin Board (see Kitchens, p. 64) because it is inexpensive, comes in a wide range of colors and is available in wider and longer pieces than most other furnishing fabrics, which was necessary for the Cube. It also offers a very contemporary feel for any room. The plasticized fabric used for the Pocket Board (see Kitchens, p. 65) was a perfect material for this room as it is hardwearing, waterproof, and fabulously kitsch!

GLUING, SCREWING AND CLAMPING

① Glue

Wood can be glued with either regular wood glue or contact adhesive. If using contact adhesive, wipe the adhesive along one of the edges to be fixed and spray the activator onto the other. Wait for about 10–15 minutes (or follow manufacturer's instructions) then press the edges together and hold tight for 10 seconds. The joint will set immediately. This method does not allow for repositioning and will not require clamping. You will only need to use clamps when using wood glue, as it takes up to 4 or 5 hours to set. Clamps are also not needed for projects using a higher gauge timber e.g., the Shadow Table (see Living Rooms, p. 28).

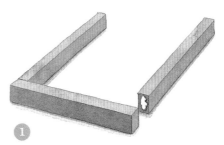

② Screw

For all the projects we recommend that you use countersunk screws (those with a flat head), so that they aren't raised above the outer surface of the wood. For the screws to be set within the wood or mdf you will need to drill pilot holes for the screws, using a hand drill with a countersink (or pilot) bit. If you require a completely flush outer surface, e.g. for the Shadow Square projects (see Living Rooms, pp. 28–29), apply a filler over the screw head and when dry, sand down.

③ Clamp

We used sash cramps to clamp all our projects, since their great length offers more strength to the kinds of joints that these projects require. If you used g-clamps, the joints would ultimately be pushed out of line because the pressure is being applied in the wrong place. When using wood glue and clamps, first drill pilot holes for the screws, apply glue to the pieces of wood/mdf as necessary and press them together, then screw to fix in position, fix the clamps, and leave overnight.

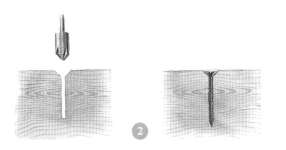

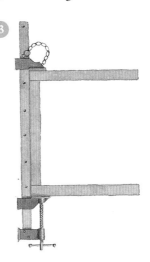

SHELF SUPPORTS

Some form of support is necessary for every kind of shelf or shelving system. There are many different types of support, which will offer you variations in load-bearing, color and aesthetic, so do think about what you will be using your shelf for and whether you require invisible supports. When buying supports be guided by the manufacturer as to the weight they can bear. Remember also the material of your wall and what kind of weight it can take (see Planning Ahead, p. 88).

① *L-shaped*

This is a metal shelf support at a 90° angle, which is screwed both to wall and shelf. Mainly made of metal, and available in a variety of sizes, these are highly visible and fairly utilitarian looking.

② *Cantilever*

Usually made of metal, these are screwed to the wall and the shelf is secured into the rebate. If using these, follow the manufacturer's instructions. These are not as visible as the L-shaped supports and can be chosen to complement the color/style of your shelf and room.

③ *Rack shelf supports*

Vertical bars, with rows of support holes, are screwed to the wall, and the shelf supports can be clipped into the corresponding holes at any height. These are versatile as they allow for different depths of shelves, and for shelves to be moved up or down at will, but they are highly visible.

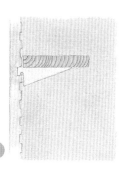

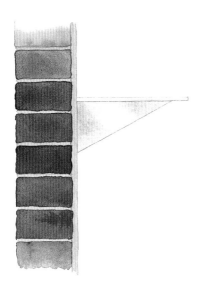

4 *Triangle*

This is the method used for Perspex Clothing System (see Bedrooms, p. 43). Cut a triangle of your chosen material at an angle of 90°, so that one side is flat against the wall and the other is flat against the shelf. The depth of the support does not have to be the same depth as the shelf, but the wider the depth the more support you will have, so it is best to think about what you will be storing on the shelf. Using contact adhesive (for plastic), glue the support to the underside of your shelf, positioning one support at each outside edge, and when dry, glue the shelf to the wall. You can use this method with different materials, but if using wood you will need to screw, as well as glue, the supports to both the shelf and the wall.

5 *Wooden dowel or metal rod*

These dowels are inserted into both the wall and the shelf, and should only be used on a very strong wall. Depending on the length of your shelf you may need to use two, three, or four dowels or rods, at equidistant points along the shelf. For each dowel, drill a hole in the wall to the exact width of dowel or rod and about 2 in. (50 mm.) deep. Drill a corresponding hole into the edge of the shelf to the required depth (the longer the dowel the more support the shelf will have). Cut your dowel or rod to the required length, remembering to include the 2 in. (50 mm.), which will go into the wall. Insert the dowel into the shelf, using a hammer to tap it into place. Once the dowel has gone as far as it can into the shelf, insert the other end of the dowel into the relevant hole in the wall, and again tap the shelf into position.

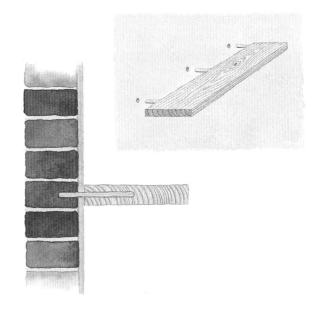

6 *Wooden dowel with batten*

You can also use dowels as an extra support when using a batten beneath a shelf (see below). Use small pieces of dowel, which can be bought in packets from hardware stores. Drill a hole in the top of the batten and a corresponding hole in the bottom of the shelf, using a drill bit of the correct length, and glue the dowel into the hole in the batten. Press the shelf into position and tap it down, so that the top of the dowel is fixed inside.

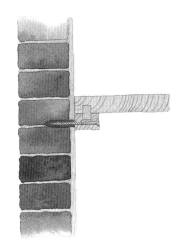

7 *Internal batten*

This can be used for an invisible support on a shelf which has an interior void, as the batten is placed inside the shelf. This method is only suitable for solid wall fixing and is used for the Desk Shelving (see Work Spaces, p. 74). Cut a

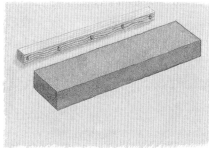

batten to suit the thickness of the shelf less twice the depth of the mdf, e.g. if the shelf is 4 in. (100 mm.) deep and the wood/mdf is ¾ in. (18 mm.), the batten should be 4 in. (100 mm.) minus 1½ in. (36 mm.), which is 2¾ in. (64 mm.). Once it is cut to size, drill the batten securely to the wall in the desired position. If the shelf is to fit inside an alcove, you can add battens to the sides of the alcove for even more support. Slide the shelf onto the battens and screw them together from underneath.

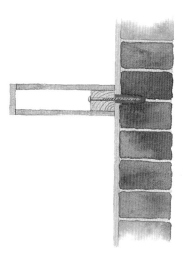

8 *External wooden batten*

For a more visible option, which can be used for shelves of less depth, use the batten as a support underneath the shelf, rather than inside. If this is being used for a large unit, such as the Pigeonholes (see Work Spaces, p. 77), additional support is required; for the Pigeonholes we used double-screw picture hangings (see p. 94).

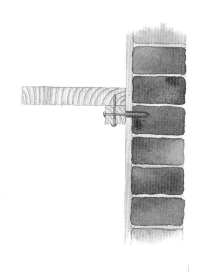

PICTURE HANGINGS

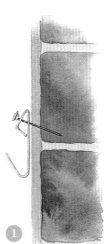

1 *Hooks*

One of the most regularly used invisible hangings, with one hook fixed to the back of the frame, and the other hook attached to the wall.

2 *Hook and wire*

Fix the hook to the wall and attach the wire on each side of the frame at the back. This hanging will be invisible if you use a short enough wire.

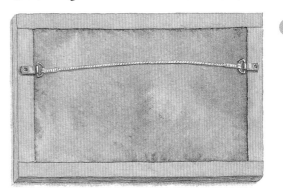

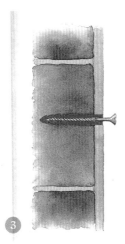

3 *Plug hook*

For an easy and invisible fixing for a light picture, drill a pilot hole in the wall to a depth suitable for the screw and tap in a wall plug. Fix the screw into the plug, leaving some of the screw protruding so that the picture can be hooked over it. Fix a small hook to the back of the frame and hook it over the screw.

4 *Double screw*

Screw the fixing to the back of the frame using the lower holes, and then screw the fixing to the wall using the upper hole. These will take the heaviest loads, but the top of each fixing is visible.

USING TRACK

Track is site specific and you will need upper and lower tracking in identical lengths. We used aluminum track for our Sliding Screen (see Halls & Corridors, p. 84).

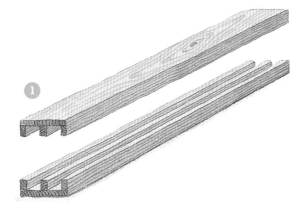

1 The shallower track is the bottom track, the deeper track is the top, designed to allow you to fit doors or screens of the correct size without them either falling out of the track or jamming.

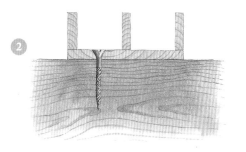

2 On the bottom track, countersink your fixings so that they are flush with the floor to ensure the smooth running of the door or screen. This type of track will only work with a lightweight screen or door. If you decide to use a more substantial material, consider using top-hung, ball-bearing sliding track for smooth operation, which is available in different styles to suit all weights of doors from most hardware or home stores.

PROJECT DIMENSIONS

It is important to take accurate measurements for each piece. The proportionate measurements of all the pieces in each project must be maintained even if you want to make the project larger or smaller than those in the book. This is particularly crucial if you are asking someone else to cut your pieces for you—check and recheck your measurements before ordering the work or you risk making a costly and frustrating mistake!

Shadow Table (see Living Rooms, p. 28)
Made from ½ in. (12 mm.) sheet birch ply (but could be mdf, which would need to be painted or varnished). You will need four identical pieces measuring 20 in. (500 mm.) square.

Shadow Shelf (see Living Rooms, p. 29)
Made from ¾ in. (18 mm.) mdf. The shorter box requires two vertical pieces of the same length and depth (ours measured 20 x 12 in. [500 x 300 mm.]), plus two horizontal pieces the same depth (12 in. [300 mm.]) by 28 in. (700 mm.) length. The longer box requires horizontal pieces of 12 in. (300 mm.) square and two vertical pieces of 28 x 12 in. (700 x 300 mm.).

Bath Shelf (see Bathrooms, p. 52)
Made from ½ in. (12 mm.) mdf. You will need two pieces cut to the length of your alcove x 12 in. (300 mm) deep, plus one facia or trim strip the length of your alcove x 8 in. (200 mm.).

Shelving Unit Room Divide (see Bedrooms, p. 42)
Made from 1 in. (24 mm.) plywood. The top, bottom and two sides of the unit were each 2 yd. x 20 in. (2 m. x 500 mm.). The four horizontal internal shelves were 1 yd 34 in. x 20 in. (1.952 m. x 500 mm.). The twenty vertical internal battens were each 15 x 20 in. (388 x 500 mm.). The ⁵⁄₃₂ in. (4 mm.) hardboard backing, which was used on the back of some of the shelves, was cut to fit – you will need to decide how many (if any) of the shelves will need this backing and cut the hardboard to the required size before nailing or screwing it onto the back of the unit as necessary.

Perspex Clothing System (see Bedrooms, p. 43)
The rod had a diameter of ¼ in. (5 mm.) and was 12 in. (300 mm.) in length. The sheet Perspex we used was ¾ in. (20 mm.) thick and the shelf supports were cut from the sheet once the two shelves had been cut to size. The upper shelf was 1 yd. x 16 in. (1 m. x 400 mm.). The lower shelf was 1 yd. x 20 in. (1 m. x 500 mm.).

Desk Shelving (see Work Space, p. 74)
The mdf for the desk should be at least ¾ in. (18 mm.) thick, the rest can be less, but should be at least ½ in. (12 mm.) thick. All pieces should be the length of your wall or alcove. For the desk, you will need two pieces 24 in. (600 mm.) wide, plus a facia/trim strip measuring 8 in. (200 mm.). For each shelf, the top and bottom pieces measured 12 in. (300 mm.) in width and the facia/trim strip measured between 4–16 in. (100–400 mm.) in width.

Pigeon Holes (see Work Space, p. 77)
Made from ¾ in. (18 mm.) mdf. The single large back piece measured 48 in. (1200 mm.) square, six other pieces (top, bottom, sides and two inner horizontal shelves) measured 48 x 14 in. (1200 x 350 mm.), the six shelf dividers measured 16 x 14 in. (400 x 350 mm.) to fit between the horizontal shelves for division and extra support.

Cube Seat (see 3 Space Saving Ideas, p. 27)
Made from ¾ in. (18 mm.) mdf. The four sides measured 20 in. (500 mm.) square each, the top and the bottom pieces measured 19¼ in. (482 mm.) square each.

PROJECT TECHNIQUES

Building a Shadow Square

This method can be used to make the basic "square" used in the shadow shelf and shadow table projects.

1 Assemble the square one piece at a time: As the corners are not mitered on these boxes, you need to make sure that when you assemble your square, the pieces that will form the top and bottom are fixed on top and underneath the side pieces to give maximum strength.

2 Apply a suitable glue to the edge of the piece you wish to attach and, ensuring that the pieces are joined at 90°, clamp into position using sash cramps (see p. 90).

4 Screw in each of the screws and counter sink.

3 Drill three pilot holes along each of the corners, one in the center, and the remaining two at an equal distance (approximately ⅜ in. [3cm.]) from each edge.

5 Fill over the countersunk screw heads with wood filler. When dry, sand the filler down, along with the rest of the piece if necessary, wipe with a cloth, and then paint.

Building a Cube

As with the shadow square, the corners on this cube are not mitered and so you need to ensure that you have fixed the pieces together to give maximum strength to the completed cube (see Building a Shadow Square, step 1, p. 97).

Put one of the larger pieces of mdf aside, as this will be used as the lid of the cube.

1 Make two L-shapes from the four side pieces. Apply wood glue to the edges, and screw to fix in position.

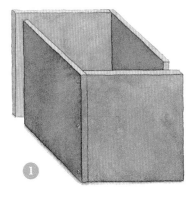

2 Apply wood glue and attach these two L-shapes together to form an open cube.

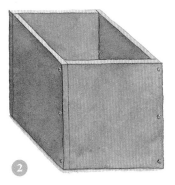

3 Drill pilot holes, at regular intervals, around the edge of the piece of wood that will become the base, remembering to drill the center hole in each side at least ½ in. (9 mm.) deep.

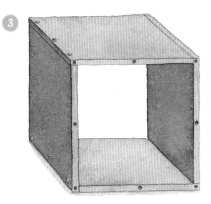

4 Apply glue to the bottom surfaces of the open cube and press the base into position. Screw the base into position using the pilot-drilled holes.

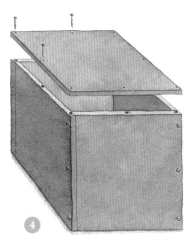

Upholstering a cube

For the lid:

 Cut wadding to cover the top of the lid and stick it down with spray adhesive.

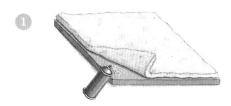

 Adding 3cm. extra all around for the hem, cut your chosen fabric to the size of your lid.

 Keeping the fabric taut at all times, smooth the fabric over the padded lid and staple it to the underside.

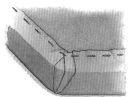

For the cube:

Cut a piece of wadding for each of the sides, each very slightly smaller than the side they are to cover so that the edges are kept sharp, and stick them down with spray adhesive. Place the fabric good side down with the cube on its side on top of it, leaving a generous hem of fabric at top and bottom.

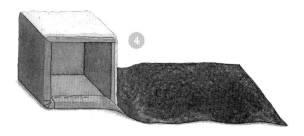 Tuck the top hem into the mouth of the box and staple down. Tuck the bottom hem under the base of the box and staple down. Roll the box over to fix the next side, and continue in the same way.

 On the last corner, cut the fabric where it meets the fabric already fixed. Oversew the seam at this corner so that the box is completely covered.

Suppliers

Ace Hardware
(630) 990-6600
www.acehardware.com
Call for store locations.
- *Hardware and shelving*

B & B Italia
(800) 872-1697
Call for store locations.
- *Built-in storage systems*

Bed, Bath & Beyond
(800) GO-BEYOND
www.bedbath&beyond.com
Call for store locations.
- *Fixtures, shelving, and storage systems.*

California Closets
(800) 336-9178
Call for store locations.
- *Custom-designed closets*

Cost Plus
(800) 777-3032
www.costplus.com
Call for store locations.
- *Imported fixtures, accessories, and decorative shelving*

Crate & Barrel
(800) 606-6387
www.crateandbarrel.com
Call for catalog and store locations.
- *Fixtures, shelving, and boxes*

Hold Everything
(800) 421-2264
Call for catalog or store locations.
- *Large selection of shelving, and storage systems*

Home Depot
(800) 430-3376
www.homedepot.com
Call for store locations.
- *Fixtures, shelving, hardware, and building supplies*

HomeLife
(800) 733-STYLE
www.ehomelife.com
- *Fixtures, shelving, and storage systems*

Houles-USA
Los Angeles, California
(310) 652-6171
- *Decorative hardware*

Ikea
(800) 959-3349
www.ikea.com
Call for store locations.
- *Fixtures, shelving, accessories, and storage units*

Interlubke
(518) 945-1007
Athens, New York
- *Open and closed shelving and entertainment storage systems*

Kmart
(800) 355-6388
www.bluelight.com
Call for store locations.
- *Fixtures, hardware, and storage accessories*

Levenger
(800) 544-0880
- *Wood file cabinets and bookcases*

Manhattan Cabinetry
(800) 626-4288
Long Island City, New York
- *Custom cabinets*

Metropolitan Shelving
(800) 992-1776
Call for store locations.
- *Distributor of classic metal shelving*

Orchard Supply Hardware
(800) SHOP-OSH
www.osh.com
Call for store locations.
- *Hardware, paints*

Pier One Imports
(800) 245-4595
www.pierone.com
Call for store locations.
- *Imported fixtures, shelving, and storage accessories*

Poliform
(212) 421-1220
www.poliform.com
- *Contemporary storage systems*

Pottery Barn
(800) 659-5507
www.potterybarn.com
Call for store locations.
- *Fixtures, accessories, and small storage systems*

Renovator's Supply
Conway, New Hampshire
(800) 659-2211
- *Decorative hardware*

Restoration Hardware
(800) 762-1005
www.restorationhardware.com
- *Decorative hardware, fixtures, and storage accessories*

Sears
(800) 544-4828
www.sears.com
Call for store locations.
- *Storage fixtures, hardware, and accessories*

Superior Shelving Systems
(253) 380-8091
Tacoma, WA
www.superiorshelving.com
- *Industrial-style wire shelving*

Target
(888) 304-4000
www.target.com
- *Basic shelving, fixtures, and storage accessories*

Techline
6333 University Avenue
Madison, WI
(608) 238-6868
www.techlinemadison.com
- *Contemporary cabinetry*

Index

Author's acknowledgments

Thank you to the very charming Richard Foster and team, especially Caroline, for the fabulous photographs, to Mick Connoly for his practical help and invaluable technical advice. To Jonty, glamorous assistant, and Louise for her project making. To Helen for her great eye, and the super-literate Nicki at Quadrille.

Publisher's acknowledgments

Thanks to those who gave permission for their photographs to appear in this book.

1 The Interior Archive/Inside Stock Image Production/W Waldron; 2 Narratives/Polly Wreford/The Holding Company; 5 Paul Ryan/International Interiors/designer Paul Pasman; 6 *Marie Claire Maison*/Nicolas Tosi/Catherine Ardouin; 8 left Ray Main/Mainstream/architect Andrew Martin; 8 right Red Cover/Winifried Heinze; 9 Henry Bourne; 10 Ray Main/Mainstream; 11 View/Peter Cook; 12 left © *World of Interiors*/Fritz von der Schulenberg; 12 right Camera Press/*Zuhause Wohnen*; 13 Arcaid/Earl Carter/*Belle*/architect Bob Nation/stylist Zinta Jurjans-Heard; 14 © *Elle Decoration*/Chris Everard; 15 Arcaid/Earl Carter/*Belle*/architect Stuart Rathe; 16 Richard Foster; 18 © *World of Interiors*/Bill Batten; 19 *Marie Claire Maison*/Nicolas Tosi/Catherine Ardouin; 20 View/Dennis Gilbert/architects James Melvin & Gollins Melvin Ward & Partners; 21 above Ray Main/Mainstream/Mathmos; 21 below *The Times*, London/Tim Clinch/architect Wells Mackereth; 22-23 Richard Glover/architect Arthur Collin; 23 Narratives/Jan Baldwin; 24-25 The Times, London/Tim Clinch/architect Wells Mackereth; 26 View/Peter Cook/architect Jonathan Woolf; 27 above Deidi von Schaewen; 27 below Richard Foster; 28 Richard Foster; 30 Ray Main/Mainstream; 31 Deidi von Schaewen; 32 Mark Seelen/architect Francis d'Haene; 33 Paul Ryan/International Interiors/designer Jacqueline Morabito; 34 Red Cover/Ken Hayden; 35 left The Interior Archive/Tim Beddow/designer Kathryn Ireland; 35 right Richard Glover/Circus Architects; 36-37 The Interior Archive/Eduardo Munoz/architect Ruben & Coque; 38-9 Narratives / Polly Wreford / The Holding Co; 40 Marie Claire Maison/Francis Amiand; 41 above Deidi von Schaewen; 41 below Verne Fotografie/architect B Declerck; 42 Arcaid/Trevor Mein/ Belle; 43 Richard Foster 44 Richard Davies/architect John Pawson; 45 Richard Davies/ Spencer Fung Architects; 46 above Christian Sarramon; 46 below Arcaid/Richard Bryant/Spencer Fung Architects; 47 Ray Main/Mainstream; 48 Ray Main/IMainstream/Martin Lee Associates; 49 Ed Reeve/architects Adjaye & Russell; 50 Arcaid/Earl Carter/*Belle*/designer Shane Chandler; 51 above Narratives/Polly Wreford; 51 below Narratives/Polly Wreford/The Holding Company; 52-53 Richard Foster; 54 Christophe Kicherer/Jane Withers (Greville Washington); 55 Ray Main/Mainstream/Isokon; 56 left Lars Ranek; 56 right Arcaid/Trevor Mein/Belle/architect John Wardle; 57 © *Elle Decoration*/Alexia Silvagni; 58-59 Undine Pröhl/architect David Baker; 60 Richard Glover/architect John Pawson; 61 left Paul Ryan/International Interiors/architect David Ling; 61 right Arcaid/Alberto Piovano/architect Kris Mys; 62 Ray Main/Mainstream/architect Sabiha Foster; 63 above Red Cover/James Merrell; 63 below Red Cover/Winfried Heinze; 64-65 Richard Foster; 66 Henry Bourne/architect Felicity Bell; 67 Ray Main/Mainstream; 68 Marie Claire Maison/Gilles de Chabaneix/Daniel Rozensztroch; 69 Ray Main/Mainstream; 70 Tim Street-Porter; 71 Ray Main/Mainstream; 72 © *Elle Decoration*/Achim Lippoth; 73 above Camera Press/Brigitte; 73 below *Marie Claire Maison*/Nicolas Tosi; 74-77 Richard Foster; 78 Richard Davies/architects Adjaye & Russell; 79 The Interior Archive/Eduardo Munoz/architect Ruben & Coque; 80 Arcaid/Earl Carter/*Belle*/architect Andrew Nolan; 81 above Louise Bobbé/architect Lucy Marsden; 81 below Ed Reeve/IPC International Syndication/ © *Living Etc*.; 82 *Marie Claire Maison*/Gilles de Chabaniex/Catherine Ardouin; 83 above Arcaid/Nicholas Kane/design by Maxwell Fry, remodelled by Ash & Sakula; 83 below Narratives/Jan Baldwin; 84 Richard Foster; 85 The Interior Archive/Christl Rohl; 86 Richard Foster.